ORGAN TRANSPLANTATION

REVISED AND UPDATED

science at the edge

ANN FULLICK

Heinemann
LIBRARY

www.heinemann.co.uk/library

Visit our website to find out more information about **Heinemann Library** books.

To order:

 Phone 44 (0) 1865 888066

 Send a fax to 44 (0) 1865 314091

 Visit the Heinemann Bookshop at www.heinemann.co.uk/library to browse our catalogue and order online.

Heinemann Library is an imprint of Capstone Global Library Limited, a company incorporated in England and Wales having its registered office at 7 Pilgrim Street, London, EC4V 6LB – Registered company number: 6695582

"Heinemann" is a registered trademark of Pearson Education Limited, under licence to Capstone Global Library Limited

Edited by Pollyanna Poulter and Claire Throp
Designed by Philippa Jenkins and Artistix
Original illustrations © Capstone Global Library
    Limited by Art Construction
Picture research by Ruth Blair
Production by Victoria Fitzgerald
Originated by Chroma Graphics (Overseas)
    Pte. Ltd
Printed and bound in China by South China
    Printing Company Ltd.

ISBN 978 0 431124 91 9 (hardback)
13 12 11 10 09
10 9 8 7 6 5 4 3 2 1

British Library Cataloguing-in-Publication Data
Fullick, Ann, 1956-
Organ transplantation. - 2nd ed. - (Science at the edge)
1. Transplantation of organs, tissues, etc. - Juvenile literature 2. Transplantation of organs, tissues, etc. - Moral and ethical aspects - Juvenile literature
I. Title
617.9'54
A full catalogue record for this book is available from the British Library.

Acknowledgements
We would like to thank the following for permission to reproduce photographs: © Alamy p. **33** (Olaf Doering); © Amanda Sheehan p. **42**; © Corbis pp. **20**, **26**, **34**, **39** (Presbyterian St. Luke's/epa), **46**, **47** (Daniel Boschung/Zefa), **57** (Pascal Rossignol/Reuters); © Lucy Sheehan p. **44**; © Michael Kienitz p. **51**; © Popperfoto pp. **16**, **18**, **41**; © Science Photo Library pp. **5**, **8** (Martin Dohrn), **10** (Edelmann), **11** (Arthur Glauberman), **12** (Garry Watson), **15** (Sheila Terry), **23**, **28** (Biology Media), **31** (Custom Medical Stock Photo), **32** (Alfred Pasieka), **37** (Cordelia Molloy), **50** (Dr Yorgos Nikas), **53** (Keith/Custom Medical Stock Photo); © Still Pictures pp. **4**(Pierre Gleizes), **21** (Mike Schroder); © Topham Picturepoint p. **46**.

Cover photograph of an x-ray of a heart reproduced with permission of © Science Photo Library.

We would like to thank David Wright for his invaluable help in the preparation of this book.

Every effort has been made to contact copyright holders of material reproduced in this book. Any omissions will be rectified in subsequent printings if notice is given to the Publishers.

CONTENTS

Some words are printed in bold, **like this**. You can find out what they mean by looking in the glossary.

THE ORGANS OF THE BODY

The human body is a masterpiece of biology. It enables us to move around to get food, escape danger, get to school on time, play football, baseball, cricket... More than that, the human body uses the food that we eat and turns it into more body or even new human beings. The body can get rid of poisons that may be taken in or are even produced by the body itself. It can survive in an enormous range of conditions, use tools, write books – and all these things are possible because of the complex biology going on inside it.

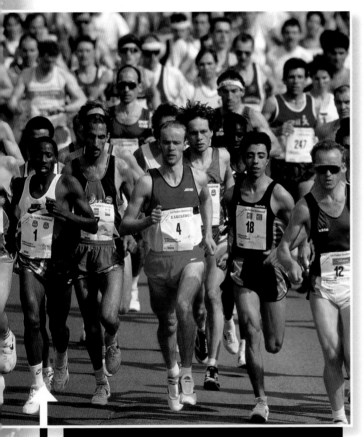

The average human being contains billions of cells, kilometres of tubing, square metres of skin, litres of fluid, and kilograms of muscle. Somehow all of this body-stuff has to be organized so that it can work properly, whatever demands are put on the body.

All of the activities of the body are made possible by major organs (collections of cells and **tissues** that carry out a major function in the body) working together to produce a co-ordinated whole. Each organ carries out a very specific job within the body. These major organs include the heart, which pumps the blood around the body, the **kidneys**, which balance the water levels in the body and get rid of waste, the eyes, which enable us to see, and the liver, which cleans and purifies the blood. The organs work together to maintain steady conditions inside the body, regardless of how it is being used or where it is.

What if things go wrong?

Almost everyone takes their body for granted – until something goes wrong. And if anything does go wrong with any of a person's major organs, they are in deep trouble – in fact the failure of a major organ can mean death. However, since the mid-1950s, there has been an enormous increase in the number of people who survive the total failure of one of their body organs, thanks to the development of transplant surgery or organ transplantation. This involves giving a very sick person the healthy organs they need from someone else, often someone who has died very suddenly. There are many thousands of people around the world who are only alive and well today because they have someone else's heart, kidney, liver, lungs, or small intestine working away inside their body, carrying out the important job that their own organ was no longer able to do.

The idea that a complex organ like the heart can be removed and replaced with another one would have seemed completely unbelievable 100 years ago. Yet now, every few minutes, someone somewhere in the world receives a transplanted organ!

How does the organization work?

The basic unit of a human being is a single cell – a jelly-like blob contained in a **membrane**. A cell carries out many chemical reactions at the same time. In large organisms, such as human beings, cells are often very specialized. This means they carry out one particular job. The structure of these cells is different from the "basic model" in order to suit the very specialized jobs that they do.

The specialized cells are often grouped together to form a tissue. In human beings, connective tissue joins bits of the body together, while nervous tissue carries information around the body, and muscle tissues move the body about.

A "typical" simple animal cell

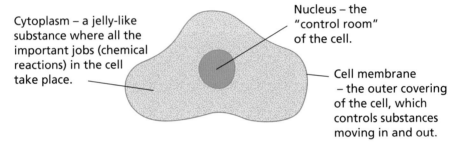

Cytoplasm – a jelly-like substance where all the important jobs (chemical reactions) in the cell take place.

Nucleus – the "control room" of the cell.

Cell membrane – the outer covering of the cell, which controls substances moving in and out.

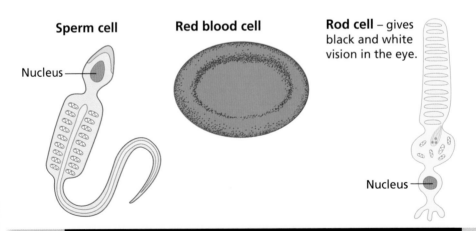

Sperm cell

Nucleus

Red blood cell

Rod cell – gives black and white vision in the eye.

Nucleus

Sometimes cells become so specialized that they only have one function within the body. Good examples of this include sperm, red blood cells, and the specialized cells involved in colour vision in the human eye (rod cells).

Cell
(for example, epithelial (lining) cell)

Whole organism
(for example,
a person)

Tissue
(for example, epithelium – thin layer
of cells lining the trachea (windpipe)

Organ
(for example, trachea)

Organ system
(for example, respiratory system)

Human body organs are made up of groups of specialized cells.
The organ systems are designed to carry out very specific jobs, for
example, getting oxygen into the blood, pumping blood around
the body, or hearing what is going on in the environment.

In many living organisms, including human beings, there is another
level of organization – several different tissues work together to form
an organ such as the heart, the kidneys, or the liver. Each of these
organs has its own job. In turn, different organs are combined in **organ
systems** to carry out major functions in the body, such as transporting
blood or reproduction. A look at the work of some of the human
organs and organ systems makes it all too clear why it is such a disaster
if they go wrong.

The heart and lungs

The heart and lungs are both vital for life, and they work together as a team, along with many kilometres of tubing called blood vessels. The heart is one of the earliest organs to be formed in the developing human **embryo**.

The heart is basically a bag of muscle that beats from a few weeks after a human embryo is formed in the **uterus** until death. It fills and empties, forcing blood out of the heart to where it is needed. The right-hand side of the heart sends blood to the lungs to pick up oxygen. At the lungs, the blood also gets rid of the poisonous **carbon dioxide** that has built up as a waste product in the working cells of the body. The left-hand side of the heart sends oxygen-rich blood, which has been through the lungs, around the rest of the body, supplying all the cells with the oxygen they need for life.

Inside every person are many different organs, all doing important jobs that help to keep us alive.

The heart is made up of muscle tissue that has its own rich blood supply. It also contains special tissue that makes up the valves of the heart (flaps that stop blood flowing in the wrong direction) and big blood vessels connect to it, which allow blood to flow into and out of the heart.

The lungs take the blood and move it around specially adapted tiny **air sacs**. These make it possible for as much oxygen as possible to be picked up by the blood, and as much carbon dioxide as possible to be removed from the blood. The process is known as gaseous exchange, and it must take place efficiently if someone is to lead a healthy, active life.

A pair of kidneys

Urea is a poisonous waste product that results from the breakdown of excess **protein** in the diet. The kidneys remove urea and excess salts from the system, and control the water balance of the body. This is enormously important – if the water balance goes wrong, all the cells in the body are in danger of either swelling or shrivelling up. Either way, they wouldn't work properly and death would not be far away!

Some organs, like lungs and kidneys, come in pairs – but why? It might be because these organs are so important they have a kind of "built-in spare". But if that is so, why do we only have one heart? No one is quite sure.

What does a liver do?

Most people know that they have a liver, but they are often unsure about where it is and what it does. The liver is one of the most important organs in the body – it carries out around 500 different jobs! It is involved in the control and management of the **carbohydrates**, proteins, and fats we eat. It helps to remove and break down **cholesterol** and other fats and convert them into storage **molecules**. It breaks down excess proteins into urea (which can be excreted) and useful amino acids, which are the chemical building blocks of proteins. It stores a number of substances, makes bile (a liquid that helps in digestion), helps control the body temperature, and breaks down some of the **toxins** taken into the body. This happens on a regular basis, because commonly used substances such as alcohol and painkillers are toxins. In fact, the liver acts like a personal detoxification (poison-removal) plant, getting rid of harmful chemicals. A liver is therefore a very useful organ to have, and when the liver fails, the body is affected in a number of ways, several of which can lead to death.

ORGAN FAILURE!

Most people are born with a set of perfectly healthy organs, which then go on to work throughout their lives. After 70, 80, 90, or even 100 years, a person's heart, kidneys, lungs, and liver may all still be carrying out the tasks for which they developed so many years earlier. However, not everyone is so lucky. Organ systems can be damaged in a number of ways, or may stop functioning altogether, for a number of reasons. The effect this has on the person concerned ranges from distressing, for example when sight or hearing is lost because of damage to the eyes or ears, through to life-threatening, for example when an organ such as the heart, liver, or kidneys fail.

Problems can start even before a person is born. Sometimes organs do not form properly as the embryo develops. If the problem shows up on an ultrasound **scan** (a technique that uses very high frequency sound to see inside the body during pregnancy) then the doctors and parents are prepared. If surgery is possible, it is done shortly after birth. Sometimes it can even take place while the baby is still developing in the uterus.

While a baby is developing in the uterus, many of its main body functions are dealt with by the mother's body, through the **placenta**. If its heart or lungs do not work properly it is not greatly affected. But after birth, the baby can be in real trouble – indeed babies die on a regular basis because of faulty organs that have failed to develop in the uterus.

Babies born after this type of surgery heal so well, they are even born without a scar! But even with the modern technology available today, babies are still born with unexpected organ problems, particularly of the heart. When this happens, the worst case is that the baby will die before surgery can correct the problem. However, in many cases, the child can be kept alive for at least a few weeks or months, by which time a solution – corrective surgery or a transplant – may be found.

Kidney infections

Sometimes people are born with a set of perfectly healthy organs, but develop an **infection** at some stage of their life that attacks and damages an organ beyond repair. For example, if an infection in the urethra (the tube that carries urine from the bladder out of the body) is neglected, the infection can spread up into the bladder and on into the kidneys, causing kidney damage and even kidney failure. Although many kidney infections are easily treated with antibiotics, repeated infections over the years or sudden very severe infections can both result in kidney failure. Without the kidneys, urea quickly builds up to toxic levels and the water balance of the body is lost. Death will occur a few days after the kidneys fail.

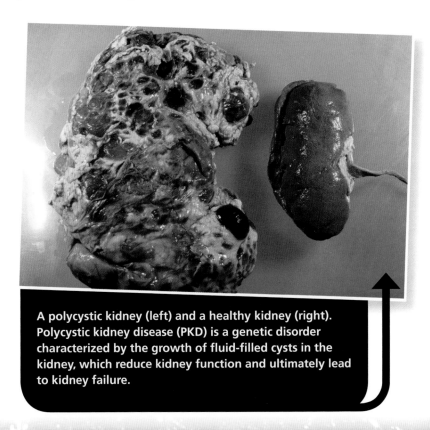

A polycystic kidney (left) and a healthy kidney (right). Polycystic kidney disease (PKD) is a genetic disorder characterized by the growth of fluid-filled cysts in the kidney, which reduce kidney function and ultimately lead to kidney failure.

Other infections

The kidneys are not the only organs that can be affected by the invasion of **micro-organisms**. Infections of the heart can damage the heart muscle so severely that it can no longer pump the blood effectively – and a badly damaged heart can cause death even more rapidly than failing kidneys. Similarly, hepatitis, a disease that is becoming increasingly common in the developed world, causes massive destruction of the liver cells. The same thing happens if the liver is attacked by liver **cancer**, another reason why liver function is sometimes lost.

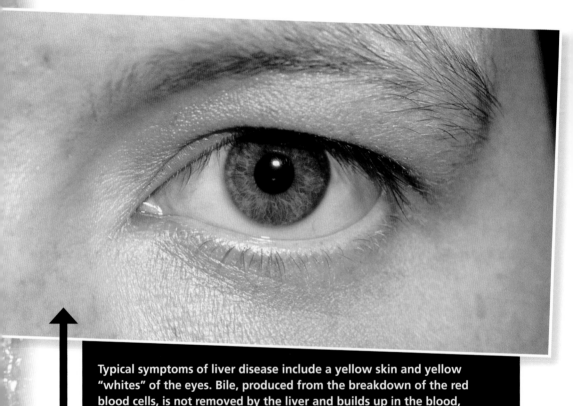

Typical symptoms of liver disease include a yellow skin and yellow "whites" of the eyes. Bile, produced from the breakdown of the red blood cells, is not removed by the liver and builds up in the blood, colouring the skin and other tissues. In contrast to the skin, the faeces lack the colour of the bile pigments, and so appear very pale. This is known as jaundice, and the level of jaundice can give an immediate indication of how well the liver is working.

The gut can also be attacked by severe infections that damage the lining so badly that it can no longer absorb food, and needs to be replaced. In the most severe infections, there is multiple organ failure. Even transplant surgery cannot help in these circumstances.

Gradual damage

Organ failure that results from severe infection does not always happen rapidly. Sometimes the destruction progresses relatively slowly, with the functioning of the organ becoming weaker over a number of years. This can be caused by progressive illnesses, such as cancer, or by damage caused by drugs. Drinking too much alcohol over a period of time can cause permanent liver damage as well as brain damage. Smoking harms the lungs, damaging the structure of the delicate air sacs and making it harder and harder to get enough oxygen into the blood. It also affects the heart, making **heart attacks** more likely. If unsuitable drugs are given to a patient, kidney and liver damage can result. High blood pressure is another common cause of damage to organs such as the kidneys. Once the filtering mechanism is damaged the organs never work properly again.

"My kidneys started to fail when I was given a drug to treat another problem. For the first nine and a half years I coped by managing my diet very carefully – I could only eat small amounts of protein and the levels of liquid and salt I took in mattered, too. But eventually I became more and more tired and began to feel really unwell."

Bernard Everard, a kidney patient, describing the gradual failing of his kidneys when he was in his fifties, after a prescribed drug for another illness caused irreversible kidney damage

Another common cause of organ damage occurs when the coronary arteries (blood vessels that supply blood to the heart) become narrowed due to a build-up of fatty deposits on the walls. If a clot then forms in the blood and blocks the blood vessel, the muscle walls of the heart are starved of oxygen and may die. The heart will stop beating. This is what is commonly known as a heart attack. Even if the patient survives the attack, if the heart is severely damaged it may never work as effectively again.

So the organs of the body can fail for a number of reasons. Problems can arise at any time from **conception** onwards, although the risk of organ failure gets higher with age. But many babies and young children also face the prospect of a much shortened life if some of their vital organs begin to fail. The challenge is to find ways to repair or replace those failing organs and give the patients back their quality of life.

"One day Christopher was playing happily with the other children – and a few days later, his life was hanging in the balance and his kidneys had failed completely. The infection struck so quickly, we were all completely stunned."

Ann Fullick, science writer, describing the speed at which a neighbour's child was affected by a kidney infection

NEW PARTS FOR OLD

For centuries, doctors have struggled to deal with the life-threatening situation of organ failure, and for most of that time there has been little or nothing they could do. Today, however, there are a number of ways of helping such patients not only to survive, but to live very healthy, active lives. One of the ways of restoring quality of life to a patient with failing organs is to give the person an organ transplant.

The history of organ transplantation goes back a very long way. People recognized that if they could replace damaged or broken body parts, many other people would be healed. But progress was very slow because successful transplants depend on a modern understanding of the immune system and how organs work together. In spite of this, some early attempts were made.

In 800 BC, there was a report in India that a surgeon called Susrata **grafted** new noses on to people using flaps of skin. From around AD 200 in China, there were reports of Hua-To replacing diseased organs with healthy ones. This seems unlikely but by using family members (or lucky tissue matches) as **donors** he may have had some success. However, there are no reports of how long the patients lived!

But genuine transplants, where a new organ is placed in the body of the **recipient** and restores them to a healthy way of life, have been a long time in coming.

The compatibility question

Before transplants could help people overcome the problems of failing organs, scientists needed a better understanding of the human body, particularly the **immune system**. This system can tell the difference between the cells of the person's body and all other cells that enter it. It will therefore reject and destroy transplanted organs because it recognizes them as different. This means that not only have scientists and doctors needed to develop surgical techniques for successful transplants, but they have also had to find ways (for example using special drugs) of preventing **rejection** of the new organ. Throughout the first 50 years of the last century, doctors and scientists were gaining in knowledge and understanding of how the organs of the body worked. They were also learning to recognize some of the signals used by the immune system.

Even in very early times, people tried to understand what was going on inside their bodies. However, their knowledge was limited to what they could find out from examining dead bodies. Over the centuries, many careful drawings of human organs were made, and understanding of the way organs worked grew. This drawing of a heart, by Leonardo da Vinci, dates from the 15th century.

Sir Peter Medawar, often known as the father of modern immunology (the study of the immune system), did a great deal of pioneering work with skin grafts during World War II, leading to a far deeper understanding of the problems of rejection.

DISCUSS   The courage to try

Carrying out the first transplants was always going to be an enormous leap in the dark. Because of the risk of trying such a new technique on a person, the patients would have to be dying. Yet if the organ transplant failed to save them the technique would be seen as a failure. Why can't doctors use patients who are not quite so ill for trying out revolutionary new treatments like this? Many people feel that patients' lives cannot be put at risk in this way. What do you think?

Transplanting kidneys

Kidneys were the first organs to be transplanted successfully. During the early 1950s, a number of experimental kidney transplants were carried out in the United States and France, but they were largely unsuccessful. In 1954, the first successful kidney transplant was carried out by Dr Joseph E. Murray in Boston, USA. The donor was the living identical twin of the patient, which meant that there were no problems with rejection. The cells of identical twins are identical, so the immune system of the twin who received the donor kidney did not recognize the new kidney as different. The transplanted kidney worked for a further eight years.

In 1959, Murray, working with his colleague Dr Merrill, performed a kidney allograft (graft from one person to another who is not genetically identical). In this case the donor and the recipient were also twins, but they were not identical twins. Another team, led by J. Hamburger in Paris, had similar success with twins. However, there were far more people who needed new kidneys than there were donors – and not many people have a convenient identical twin. Could they use the kidneys from dead donors instead of live donors?

Dr Joseph E. Murray won the Nobel Prize for Medicine in 1990, for his pioneering work on kidney transplantation. Of English and Irish origins, he began his surgical career in the United States, working on soldiers burned during World War II. This is where his interest in the problems of avoiding rejection began. His work on kidney transplantation helped make life after transplantation a reality for many thousands of people.

The ethics of using dead donors

When it comes to doing something as amazing as taking an organ out of a person who has died and putting it inside the body of another person, there are bound to be all sorts of issues associated with it.

Some people simply cannot accept the idea of part of one person being used inside another, and feel that they could never be an organ donor. Other people find the idea of the body of someone they love being divided up and organs being removed very hard to come to terms with, particularly if they only think about it when someone very close to them has died unexpectedly. Added to this there are occasional "scare stories" in the press of people taking on another personality after a transplant operation, particularly heart transplants. Other people feel that it would be against their religion, and that somehow this is interfering with God's will.

In fact, most of the main religions have no problem with organ donation. The Christian religions all see organ donation, either from a dead or living donor, as an act of compassion and giving to save life. The Churches all feel that the body of a dead donor should be treated with respect, and that organ donation should not be done for money, but within these constraints transplant surgery is seen as a good and beneficial form of medicine.

> "Don't take your organs to heaven with you. Heaven knows we need them here."
>
> Author unknown, attributed to both Dan and Barbara Hladio and Thomas Boyadjis, Sr.

The teachings of Islam also support organ donation. Saving life is of paramount importance and Muslims are allowed to both accept organ donation and to act as organ donors themselves. Whilst in an ideal world both donor and recipient would be Muslim, in practice saving all life is seen as important.

> "[...] And if anyone saved a life it would be as if he saved the life of the whole people."
>
> Qur'an ch 5 v 32

Many other religious groups also support transplantation – Hindus, Sikhs, and Buddhists all see organ donation as being totally acceptable and more than that, a positive and generous gesture.

The pioneers – making transplants a reality

In 1962, the team in Boston, USA triumphed again when they transplanted a kidney from a dead donor into a live patient. The recipient was given drugs to try to prevent rejection. The new kidney worked successfully for 21 months before it was finally rejected by the patient's body. After this, developments came thick and fast. People were trying all sorts of methods to overcome the problems of rejection. Early methods included irradiating patients (exposing them to electro-magnetic radiation) before transplant surgery to destroy their bone marrow. This was to stop the production of **lymphocytes** (white blood cells), as these would attack the new organ. The problem with the irradiation method was that patients sometimes died as a result of it, so the transplant didn't have a chance to survive. Special anti-rejection drugs were also introduced. In the early days, these were very toxic and again, the anti-rejection treatment sometimes killed the patient.

The pioneering work of people like Dr Joseph E. Murray (see page 16), Dr Thomas Starzl and Dr Christiaan Barnard paved the way for organ transplants to become a recognized way of treating patients with total organ failure. Dr Barnard is seen here carrying out an experimental operation on a dog.

In spite of the early difficulties, a floodgate had opened and new and different organ transplants were taking place every year. In 1963 the first human liver transplants took place at the University of Colorado, USA. They were carried out by Dr Thomas Starzl. However, the best survival time was only 21 days. That same year Dr James Hardy carried out the first lung transplant in Mississippi, USA. By 1966 the first successful transplant of a pancreas (an organ that makes hormones and digestive enzymes) from a dead donor had taken place. Starzl continued his work, and in 1967 his team performed the first successful liver transplants, with four of their seven patients surviving for weeks and even months.

Building on success

Heart transplants became a reality in 1967, with the work of Christiaan Barnard. After this massive step forward, there was a period during which transplant surgeons and scientists working on rejection consolidated their work. Much research was done on improving operating techniques. Anti-rejection treatment also got better and patient survival times grew longer and longer.

Then, in the 1980s, things moved forward dramatically again. The first combined heart and lung transplant took place in 1981. It was carried out by Dr Norman Shumway and Dr Bruce Reitz at Stanford University, USA. In 1988, Dr David Grant, operating in Ontario, Canada, achieved the first successful transplant of a small intestine. Since then, through the 1990s and on into the 21st century, great improvements have been made in anti-rejection drugs. This has meant that the chances of a transplant being rejected by the body of the recipient have been much reduced, and so transplant surgery has become increasingly successful.

There has also been an increase in the number of organs that it is possible to transplant at one time. Multiple-organ transplants, with up to four different donor organs being given to a single very sick patient, have become a reality – although they are still relatively rare. The most common organs to be transplanted in this way are the liver, various other **abdominal organs**, such as the small and large intestines, and the heart and lungs.

The big one – transplanting hearts

The beating of the heart is so closely associated with life that it is almost impossible to imagine that someone could have their heart removed and survive the experience. Yet this is what happened in 1967, when Dr Christiaan Barnard in Cape Town, South Africa, carried out the first ever successful human heart transplant. The patient, a middle-aged man called Louis Washkansky, was given the heart of Denise Darvall, a 23-year-old woman who had died in a car accident. The whole world was amazed at what had been achieved. Louis lived for 18 days with his new heart beating in his chest before dying of a lung infection. A second attempt, by an American team in New York, failed – the patient died after six hours. But in 1968 Phillip Blaiberg received a new heart in the second transplant carried out by Dr Barnard, and he lived to enjoy a relatively normal life for nearly two years. Nowadays, heart transplant surgery hardly even makes local headlines.

"If you can't save my daughter, you must try and save this man."

Edward Darvall, father of the donor in the first heart transplant operation. He had just lost both his wife and his daughter in the same accident when they were hit by a drunken driver

It is important to remember patients such as Louis Washkansky (left) and Phillip Blaiberg and their families. Without their bravery and the enormous generosity of the bereaved families who donated their organs, progress in this field would have been impossible.

HOW IS IT DONE?

If a battery runs out in a toy, it is easily replaced. When a light bulb stops working, it takes just a few moments to remove the old bulb and put in a new one. When organs of the body fail for whatever reason, replacing them is not nearly so simple!

When a potential donor organ becomes available, there is a great deal to do. The tissue type of the donor must be matched as closely as possible with a person needing an organ transplant. There are two operating teams working at the same time, sometimes in the same hospital, sometimes in other parts of the country or even in another country. One team removes the organs from the body of the organ donor and packs them in specially prepared boxes for transporting to the operating theatre, where they are needed for a transplant. Meanwhile, the other team will be preparing the recipient to receive their new organ.

It is important that the donor organ is ready and waiting in the operating theatre before the recipient's diseased organ is removed. The organ may have to be transported hundreds of kilometres – and speed is of the essence!

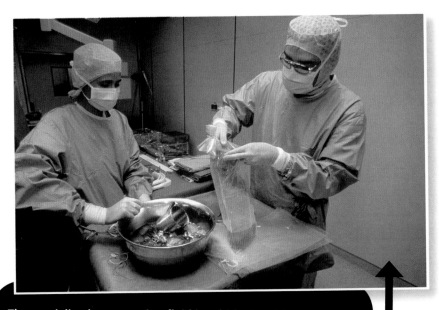

The specialized preservation fluid in which this kidney is being stored, along with low temperatures, will make sure it remains healthy while it is not functioning as part of a body.

It is vitally important that the donor organs are kept healthy and functional once they have been removed from the donor's body. This is done by washing the blood out of them using special, chilled preservation fluid, which produces a state of "suspended animation" in the organ. This means the vital functions of the organ temporarily stop, but will return when the organ is connected to a bodily system again. They are stored in this fluid, surrounded by ice, to keep them at 4°C (39°F) while they are transported to wherever they are needed. If ice actually came into contact with the tissue, it would freeze it and cause permanent damage, and the organ would be of no use.

The preservation fluids are very specialized. Research goes on all the time to improve them so that the organs can survive out of the body for longer periods of time. The fluids may cost as much as £150 per litre!

The transplant operation

Transplanting organs always involves surgery, and all surgery involves some risk to the patient. Firstly, the patient needs to be under an anaesthetic, in a chemically induced sleep, while the operation takes place, so that he or she does not feel what is going on. It often takes a long time to carry out a transplant operation – several hours at least. The patient has to be carefully monitored to make sure there are no problems, and the risk of problems arising increases the longer the patient is under the anaesthetic.

Secondly, transplant surgery involves opening up the body to take out the old organ and replace it with a new one. As with all surgery, as soon as the body is opened up, it is very vulnerable to infection. Because transplant surgery goes on for a long time, and involves introducing an organ from someone else's body, the risk is increased.

"The most exciting thing when you are working as a transplant surgeon is when you have put the new kidney in the body. You take a small, brown, cold, insignificant little thing with all the blood washed out of it from the box. You put it into your patient, connect the blood vessels – and when you remove the clamps the whole organ turns pink and expands as new life flows into it. It never stops being amazing!"

Anne M. Walters, consultant renal transplant surgeon, Wessex Renal Transplant Unit, UK

Transplant challenges

Transplanting an organ raises some particular challenges. Each organ in the body carries out specific and very important functions. In many operations, the body of the patient continues as normal whilst surgery on a particular part goes on. During a transplant, entire organs are removed, and so their function may have to be taken over by machines. This is particularly true in heart and lung transplants, because the body cannot function without the oxygen they provide. The patient is also often chilled, because at a low temperature the cells of the body need much less oxygen and sugar and they produce less waste. This means the cells are more likely to survive without any damage.

Another problem is making sure that the donor organ fits into the body of its new host. Obviously, transplants are only given when there will be a reasonable match between the size of the donor and the recipient, but even then there may still be problems. The original organ and the replacement will not be exactly the same, and neither will the blood vessels that supply them with blood. Yet these blood vessels have to be joined together in such a way that they won't leak. If the organ is much smaller or larger than the original, then this can cause problems. Once the bloodflow is allowed to return to the new organ, the doctors watch to see if the blood supply works and whether the transplanted organ seems to "come alive" in its new body.

The operating team has to maintain very high standards of cleanliness to make sure that the site of the operation does not get infected. Because transplants tend to be quite long operations, there is more opportunity for things to go wrong.

Vein
Artery
Old kidneys left in the body.
Ureter carries urine from kidney to bladder.
New kidney attached to the blood vessels and the bladder.
Urethra – tube that carries urine from the bladder out of the body.
Bladder

The normal procedure for a transplant leaves the failed kidneys in place. The new kidney is positioned lower in the body and the blood vessels of the kidney are connected to the blood vessels going to the legs, whilst the ureter, the tube from the kidney that carries urine away, is linked directly into the bladder.

Bigger and better

For many years, as transplant surgery was developed, single organs were transplanted to replace organs that had ceased to function. But over the years, transplant surgeons have developed a number of different techniques, some of which involve transplanting several organs at a time.

Sometimes transplants will be carried out when the patient's own organ still functions to a small extent. "Piggy-back" transplants may be carried out, which means that a new organ is joined to the patient's own organ so that they work together. The new stronger organ carries out most of the work, allowing the original organ to rest and in some cases to recover. If it does recover, and even if the new organ is eventually rejected and has to be removed, the patient will remain healthy.

Doctors have become increasingly ambitious in the number of organs they transplant. Very often the failure of one organ leads to problems in another. For example, lung disease can cause damage to the heart, or problems in the liver can lead to failure of parts of the digestive system. There has been a gradual increase in the transplantation of more than one organ at a time. The first successful heart/lung transplant was carried out by Dr Norman Shumway and Dr Bruce Reitz at Stanford University, USA in 1981. Since then a number of different organ combinations have been transplanted successfully, including up to four different abdominal organs at a time!

"The day after I had my transplant, I couldn't believe the effect it had on my thought processes – it was as if a fog had been lifted off my mind."

Ex-naval officer after receiving a new kidney

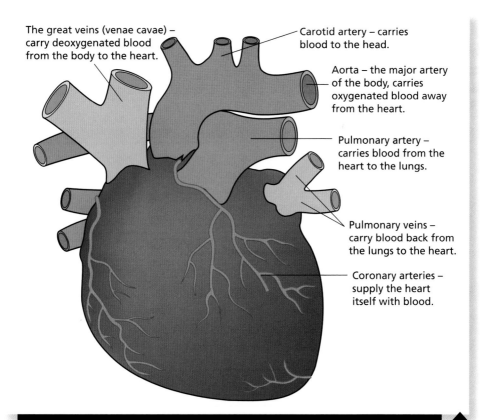

The great veins (venae cavae) – carry deoxygenated blood from the body to the heart.

Carotid artery – carries blood to the head.

Aorta – the major artery of the body, carries oxygenated blood away from the heart.

Pulmonary artery – carries blood from the heart to the lungs.

Pulmonary veins – carry blood back from the lungs to the heart.

Coronary arteries – supply the heart itself with blood.

When a heart transplant is carried out, the failing heart is removed and the new organ placed in the chest cavity. All of the massive blood vessels carrying blood back to the heart from the body, and out around the body from the heart, have to be reconnected so that blood doesn't leak out and make the new organ inefficient.

Domino transplants

Another new type of transplant surgery was developed in the USA in 1987. Sometimes a patient has damaged lungs but a perfectly healthy heart – for example with **genetic diseases** such as cystic fibrosis. Although lung transplants can be carried out and are effective in these cases, often complete heart/lung transplants are more successful. This is because the connections between the heart and the lungs do not have to be made, and the two organs are the right size for each other. These transplants are known as **domino transplants** because the healthy heart of the patient who receives the new heart and lungs is then transplanted into someone else who needs a new heart. Domino transplants are still relatively rare, but when they do take place they can be very successful.

Here, the transplant team at the hospital at Stanford University in California, USA, removes the diseased heart and the lungs from a patient.

Professor Dame Julia Polak – a heart-lung transplant success story!

Professor Julia Polak is a scientist who studied lung disease, including a rare, fatal condition called pulmonary hypertension. Then in 1995, by a cruel twist of fate, Julia was diagnosed with the same disease herself. She was given less than a year to live unless she had a complete heart and lung transplant. Amazingly, within seven weeks a suitable donor was found and Julia had her life-saving surgery. Ever since she has worked tirelessly in tissue engineering, trying to find a way of persuading stem cells to act as a lung repair kit. The aim is to produce a treatment so that new lung tissue can be developed for anyone who needs it. Julia is one of the longest surviving heart-lung transplant patients in the UK.

"After my transplant I changed the course of my research. I realised that there is an immense shortage of donor organs and wanted to find ways of reducing this. The long term aim is to create artificial organs in a test tube, but this will take a very long time to achieve successfully. Cell therapy ... is a possible alternative. Patients could remain alive for a long time, or even be cured, depending on how advanced the disease is when treated."

Professor Polak

Transplant coordinators

Whatever type of transplant is carried out, the success of the whole complex procedure depends heavily on the transplant coordinators. They are involved in supporting the recipient and their family as they prepare for the transplant, through the operation and afterwards as they recover and learn to manage the all important **immuno-suppressant** drugs. One of their most important jobs is coordinating the transplant process once a donor has been found. They make sure that everyone is in the right place at the right time and that the donor organ and the recipient are in a fit condition for the surgery to go ahead. They also work with the donor families, supporting them in their grief and helping them come to terms with events. The transplant coordinators continue their support for the donor families long after the various transplants have gone ahead. Not only this, they play an important role in educating family doctors, hospital doctors, and the general public about transplant surgery.

REJECTION!

There are many worries and problems for doctors involved in organ transplantation, and for the people who have received a transplant, whatever the type or number of organs received. But the biggest fear of all is that of rejection – when the patient's immune system begins to recognize the cells of the new life-giving organ as foreign and tries to destroy it. What is the immune system and why is it so important?

The immune system

The immune system enables individual cells within the human body to recognize each other as part of the same living thing, and to recognize other cells that carry out the same jobs so they can work together as part of a tissue or an organ. It also recognizes foreign cells – invading micro-organisms such as bacteria and viruses that might cause disease, as well as the cells of transplanted organs – as "non-self", which need to be destroyed.

Once the lymphocytes have destroyed a foreign cell, phagocytes (another type of white blood cell) move in to engulf and "eat" the dead cell. The phagocytes are like rubbish-collectors and move around clearing up after the lymphocytes. The pus you see in an infected cut is made up largely of dead phagocytes, which have taken in so many dead bacteria, it has killed them!

How the immune system works

The human body recognizes the presence of foreign antigens by means of lymphocytes. Everybody makes thousands of different lymphocytes and each lymphocyte recognizes one specific type of antigen. Lymphocytes involved in the immune response of the body are divided into two types: T-cells and B-cells. They are both made in the **bone marrow** and then move to different sites in the body where they grow and mature into T- and B-cells. When mature, the T-cells bind to foreign cells directly and destroy them whereas the B-cells make antibodies to destroy the foreign cells. A single B-cell can make up to 2000 antibody molecules per second! Once the right antibody has been made, special memory cells make sure that if the body ever comes into contact with that foreign antigen again, it can respond immediately with the right antibody.

The antigen/antibody reaction is a very clever way of making sure that the body recognizes foreign cells. However, because the antigens on the surface cells of a donor organ are different from those on the recipient's cells, the whole system backfires. In a transplant patient, the immune response can mean death rather than life.

HOW DO CELLS RECOGNIZE EACH OTHER?

On the surface of cell membranes, there are many special marker molecules known as **antigens**. Each person has some specialized antigens on the surface of their cells, which are unique to them. It is these individual markers that form the basis of the immune system and enable the body to recognize very rapidly if an organ from another person is placed inside it. Special white blood cells called lymphocytes make proteins called **antibodies**, which attach to any foreign antigens and inactivate the invading cells, which are then destroyed.

Human blood groups – another step forward

The human immune system is extremely complicated and makes life very difficult for doctors wanting to transplant organs from one person to another. For example, human beings have some unique antigens on their red blood cells, and this divides the population into different blood groups. The blood also contains antibodies that will destroy cells containing antigens it does not recognize. If some blood groups are mixed together, the antigens react with antibodies in the blood, causing the cells to stick together. This blocks blood vessels and can kill a patient. However, other blood groups can be mixed with no ill-effects. For any transplant to be successful, the blood groups of the donor and recipient must be the same or at least compatible. If not, the transplant is doomed to failure from the start. As the **ABO system** of categorizing human blood groups was not discovered until 1901, there wasn't much chance of successful transplant surgery before that time.

The immune system, which is so important in protecting the body against disease, is the worst enemy of a transplanted organ. The battle to prevent rejection has determined how successful transplant programmes have been. For many years resources were very limited and involved almost the total destruction of patients' immune systems, leaving them open to a wide range of infections. Two advances have helped to weigh the odds more strongly in favour of the patient.

Tissue typing

All people have some antigens in common. Others are specific to a particular individual. The more closely related two individuals are, the more likely they are to have lots of antigens in common. However, completely by chance, some unrelated individuals also have similar sets of antigens. However, the only people who have exactly the same antigens on their cells are identical twins, because they both came from the same **fertilized** egg and sperm.

As human understanding of the immune system has increased, so more care has been taken with matching the tissues between donor and recipient. The more similar the antigens on the donor organ are to the antigens on the cells of the recipient, the better the chances of the transplant "taking" and rejection being avoided.

In the UK and Europe, there are computer data banks of the tissue type of all the people waiting for organs. When a donor becomes available, the most suitable recipients can be found. Organs are then transported to where they are needed. Until recently, each state in the United States tended to use any available organs within that state.

Relatively recent legislation has changed this so that organs are offered to the sickest people with the best tissue match, rather than to the nearest needy patient. Unfortunately for the patients, some states are contesting this in spite of the evidence that tissue-matching is important. US research has shown that out of 7,614 people who got a perfect tissue-match transplant, 52 per cent of the organs were still working ten years later. In contrast, out of a group of 81,364 patients who had less than perfect matches, only 32 per cent of the organs were still working ten years later. So a good match makes a lot of difference.

FOCUS   Organ transportation

All too often each country – or area of a country – operates independently when it comes to finding donor organs. Yet a good match can make all the difference to the success of a transplant. Modern transport methods mean organs can be carried long distances in only a few hours. For example, if there is no suitable recipient for a donor organ in the UK, it will be offered to all the countries in Europe to see if there is a better match.

These medical staff are loading a case containing organs for transplant surgery into an ambulance. The case keeps the organs cool so that they can survive for a longer period outside a body. Organ transfers between hospitals are often needed for transplant operations.

Preventing rejection using drugs

In 1969, scientists in United States and Norway discovered a **fungus** that was to have far-reaching effects on the success of transplant surgery in the future. In 1972, Jean Borel, working in Switzerland, found that a chemical called **cyclosporine**, which could be isolated from the fungus, had immuno-suppressant properties – in other words, it damped down the reaction of the immune system. By 1980, this "wonder-molecule" had been **synthesized** for the first time, and by 1983, it was approved for commercial and clinical use. When cyclosporine is given to patients after a transplant, the risk of rejection is greatly reduced because the activity of their immune system is lowered.

Cyclosporine, particularly when used in partnership with other drugs such as some **steroids**, has had a major impact on the numbers of people having successful transplants. Transplant patients have to take their immuno-suppressant drugs for the rest of their lives, because the body would never get used to the new organ and accept it. The main downside of drugs like this is that they suppress the whole immune system, making the people taking them more vulnerable to normal infections. However, because everyone is aware of this, transplant patients are simply carefully monitored and given other medicines to help them if they develop an infectious illness.

In the last 10 years, many new drugs have been developed to help guard against rejection. Some replace cyclosporine, whilst others are used alongside it. Pharmacologists (people who study the science of drugs) are the great allies of transplant surgeons in the war against rejection!

A computer model of a molecule of cyclosporine, the amazing new immuno-suppressant drug that has enabled thousands of people to benefit from an organ transplant without rejection problems.

An immune system "miracle"

When Australian Demi-Lee Brennan was nine years old, she had a viral illness that destroyed her liver. She was hours away from death when she was given the liver transplant she needed to save her life. Like all transplant patients, Demi was given immuno-suppressant drugs to prevent her body rejecting the new organ. She made good progress until nine months later, when she became very ill again. Her doctors were completely amazed when they discovered that her blood type had changed.

Demi's donor had been blood group O positive, while Demi was O negative. But her blood group changed to become O positive. Stem cells from the new liver seemed to have invaded her bone marrow and taken over her immune system, which meant that she didn't need the immuno-suppressant drugs. The doctors daren't stop the drugs but the situation was like nothing they had ever seen before. By 2008, when she was 15 years old, Demi had been completely free of immuno-suppressants for almost four years. Research teams all over the world are interested in this "miracle" of biology. If they can discover how and why Demi's immune system changed, it might lead the way to new treatments for other transplant patients – and perhaps end the need for a lifetime on drugs.

"I feel quite normal. It's almost like it never happened. I can't thank the donor's family enough, and the doctors, for giving me this second chance at life."

Demi-Lee Brennan

After a transplant operation, a patient has to take a cocktail of drugs every day for the rest of their life to prevent their immune system from destroying their new organ.

LIFE FROM DEATH

When someone has an organ that is failing, the obvious solution is to replace it with a new one. There is one huge problem with this, however – where is the new organ going to come from?

The most common source of donor organs are people who have died. Road accidents kill 3,000 people a year in the UK alone. Many of those killed are relatively young and perfectly fit and healthy apart from the injuries – often to the brain – that kill them. Some people die from an unexpected haemorrhage (massive bleeding) in the brain, or a heart attack. Whenever a healthy person meets a sudden, unexpected death most of their organs will be in perfectly good condition. These organs can be given to someone else, someone who is dying because their heart, kidneys, liver, or another organ can no longer fulfil its function.

Every day, people leave their homes to go to work, to school, out with friends – and never return. The roads claim many lives every week, and parents, children, and partners have to come to terms with a sudden and totally unexpected loss.

Granting permission

A person who has suddenly died is obviously in no position to grant permission for their organs to be given to someone else. Yet without permission, it is illegal for doctors to remove organs from a dead body for the purpose of transplantation. What is more, if organs are to be used for transplantation, it is vital that the donor is kept on a life-support machine, so that even after they are clinically dead (all brain activity is lost), blood is pumped around their body and their organs are supplied with oxygen to keep them functioning. This is because if the body goes even a short time without oxygen, the organs will be damaged and therefore useless to anyone else. The machine takes over the functions of the heart and the lungs, getting oxygen into the blood, pumping it around the body and removing carbon dioxide.

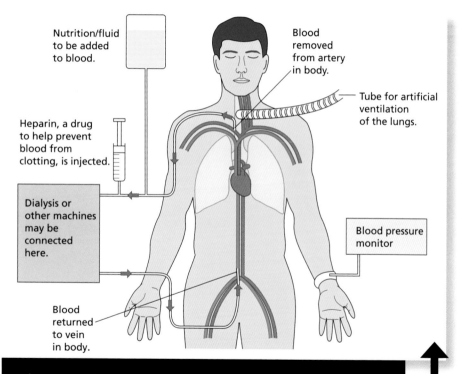

Nutrition/fluid to be added to blood.

Blood removed from artery in body.

Tube for artificial ventilation of the lungs.

Heparin, a drug to help prevent blood from clotting, is injected.

Dialysis or other machines may be connected here.

Blood pressure monitor

Blood returned to vein in body.

When an accident victim or someone who has suffered any type of medical catastrophe is brought into hospital, they will be put on a life-support machine if it is needed. This gives doctors the opportunity to assess the patient and see if there is any chance of his or her survival, and also keeps organs such as the liver and kidney functioning. If the patient's organs are to be used for transplantation, he or she will be kept on the machine even after they are found to be clinically dead, until the organs are removed.

When is death?

Doctors can only use a person's organs for transplantation if that person is dead – but how do we know when someone is dead and has no hope of recovery? In years gone by, people were judged to be dead when their heart stopped beating and they stopped breathing. Many people still think of death in this way. But in the case of sudden death, whether due to accidents or medical emergencies, machines can maintain the working of the body. In some cases, the heart keeps functioning at the level of a very basic reflex – a rapid nervous response that does not involve the **central nervous system**. In these cases, doctors have to look elsewhere for a definition of death. A patient is defined as being dead when their brain stem, the very lowest region of the brain, is dead. Once the basic regions of the brain stop functioning, the patient has no awareness, no thought, no life except that given by machines. Once a patient is certified as brain-stem dead – a process that takes a long time and several doctors – then the possibility of using the organs for transplantation becomes real.

A dreadful dilemma

When a patient is certified as dead, it is a terrible time for everyone concerned. Doctors are faced with a dreadful dilemma. If they ask the relatives – stunned, shocked, grieving – for permission to use the organs of their loved one for transplantation, then they may add to their distress. If they don't ask, then they are losing the chance of prolonging the lives of several people waiting desperately for an organ transplant. And, if the organs are to be used for successful transplants, there is no time to lose.

For the relatives, this is a hard decision to make at a difficult time, and if they have not thought about it before, then they may feel unable to "give away" part of their loved one's body. If the potential donor is on a life-support machine, then they will still be warm, appear to be breathing, and will look as if they are simply asleep, making it even harder for relatives to accept that death has occurred. If permission to use the organs is refused, the life-support machine will be switched off when it seems right to the family – usually after a few hours. If people have made it known they want to be a donor, the organs will be used almost automatically. But it is vital that people discuss their wishes with family members too, so that if the worst happens, everyone knows what to do.

Registering as a donor

There is one thing that can make the situation of organ donation easier for everyone concerned. In countries like the UK, the United States, and Australia, people can decide that if anything terrible should happen to them they would like to give life to other people. To show that this is their choice, they can register as an organ donor. In the UK this can be done in a number of ways including when people apply for a driving licence or by registering directly online and 25 per cent of the population are now registered. Similarly in the US – around 70 million people have registered with their driving licences or ID cards. In Australia there is a slightly different system, with a legally binding organ donor register where you can register that you do – or don't – want your organs to be used after death and just over a million have so far joined.

Some people also choose to carry donor cards to alert medical staff in an emergency, but with the databases accessible through computers these are becoming less necessary.

If people are registered as potential donors and are involved in an accident or taken seriously ill and die, the doctors know immediately that the organs are available for transplantation.

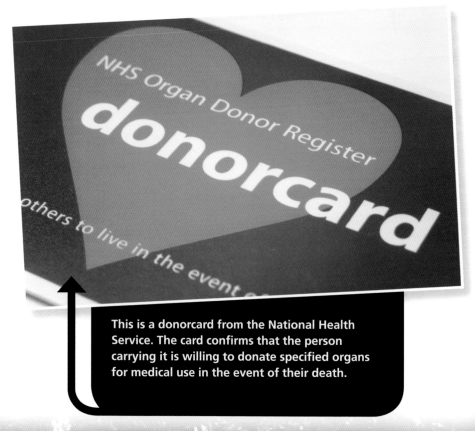

This is a donorcard from the National Health Service. The card confirms that the person carrying it is willing to donate specified organs for medical use in the event of their death.

Deciding to be a donor

If a person dies suddenly, a difficult situation is made easier if that person has previously expressed a wish to be an organ donor. However, persuading people to become potential donors and carry a donor card is not easy. People often don't want to think about the possibility of their own death. Many other people are full of good intentions but simply don't get round to registering.

Some countries now have a system where everyone is automatically assumed to be a potential organ donor. Anyone who does not want to give their organs has to opt out of this system. This has greatly increased the number of organs available for transplantation in those countries where it has been tried, such as Belgium.

In many US states, it has been made law that doctors ask the families of all potential donors if they will allow donation. This means that they cannot be accused of insensitivity at a difficult time, because they are simply obeying the law. For many other families, however, the opportunity to donate organs from their loved one's body is seen as a way of bringing something positive out of a terrible situation.

> "It is a very, very noble act – and human beings are capable of very noble acts ... They can help seven or eight other people live who are about to die – they [the family] think that something good can come out of it.'
>
> Sir Magdi Yacoub, pioneering heart transplant surgeon

> 'If anything ever happens to me I want my organs to go to someone else.'
>
> Scott Dudley (US teenager), not long before he was killed in an accident with a gun. His organs gave two people their sight (using the corneas from his eyes) and four lives were saved with his heart, kidneys, liver, and pancreas.

Living donors

While most transplants are carried out using organs removed after death, not all organ donors are dead. Live donors are an increasingly important group. Most commonly, live donors are members of the same family as the person who is suffering from organ failure.

There is obviously a limit to the number and type of organs that can be given by a living donor. The most commonly donated organs are kidneys, because everyone has two of them. An individual can get on with life perfectly well with just one kidney, although they are obviously more at risk if they ever have kidney problems themselves because they have lost their "spare". The liver can also be donated.

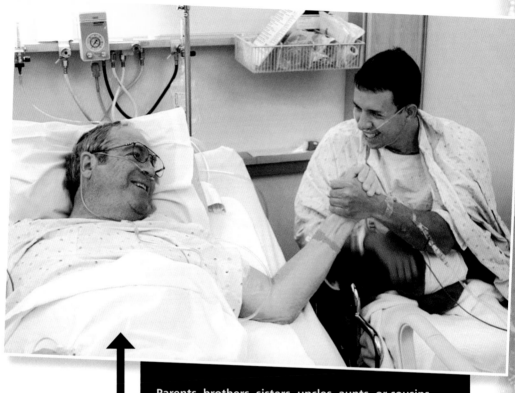

Parents, brothers, sisters, uncles, aunts, or cousins
– blood relatives have a much higher chance of giving
a very good tissue match than an unrelated donor.
Husbands and wives have also sometimes been able
to act as organ donors for each other. However,
history was made when kidney transplant patient Bob
Hickey, 58, (left) received a kidney from Robert Smitty,
32. The two men were the first patient and donor
matched through a commercial website.

Although each person has only one liver, it is a large organ that
regrows at a very rapid rate. Part of the liver can be removed from
a living donor, and blood vessels from this tissue joined to the blood
vessels supplying the recipient's liver. The liver tissue will regenerate
in both the donor and the recipient very quickly, and the transplanted
organ will take over the function of the damaged or destroyed liver.
On the other hand, organs such as the heart obviously cannot be given
by a living donor, because everyone has only one heart and needs it to
stay alive!

There are cases where living donors have swapped organs, for example, if husbands or wives want to act as a living donor for their partner but their tissues don't match. They can be paired up with another couple and the donors give their organs to someone who needs them – and both recipients get an organ that is a tissue match!

"The short term pain and discomfort I experienced was nothing compared to the pleasure of seeing the cloud of kidney disease lifted from my son."

Tim, a man from Dallas, USA, who donated a kidney to his son

DISCUSS   Ethics and issues

There are always more people needing transplants than there are suitable organ donors. Although in many countries more and more people are signing up as potential donors, the shortages remain. Living donors can help, but they are relatively few and far between. Most living donors give their organs freely either to someone they love or to someone they do not know but who has appealed for an organ as a matter of urgency.

However, sometimes the desire to have organs for donation overrides moral and **ethical** boundaries. For example, in some parts of the world, such as India, there is great poverty but also some great medical expertise. There have been many instances of people selling their organs – particularly kidneys – for use in transplantation. The people who sell their kidneys are often desperate for money to pay off debts, to pay for health care for a family member, or to feed and educate their children. A price of around £400 for a kidney might not sound much, but it is several years income to someone living in the slums of a city such as Madras.

The Indian government banned a trade in organs more than 10 years ago, but it still flourishes as an illegal trade between desperately ill people and desperately poor people, usually with a middleman making thousands of pounds out of each transaction. Many groups find this unacceptable, particularly if people are pressured to do it. It seems wrong that people

Continued ...

should compromise their own health – donating an organ is not without risk – simply for money. Others feel that if the trade was legalised and the people with organs to donate were paid a fair price, the situation could be used to benefit both sides.

What do you think? How would you feel if a member of your family desperately needed a transplant and no legal organs were available? What would you do if it was your family starving or your children not getting a good education? Would you solve the problem by selling an organ from your body?

Once money is involved, only rich people can afford transplants, and only poor people will sell their organs. Corruption is rife. Yet not enough people volunteer to be organ donors, so thousands of people die each year because they need a transplant. The choices are very hard.

In some instances there appears to be evidence that the organs of condemned criminals have been "harvested" and sold for organ donation. This practice was reported in China a few years ago. In 2006, the Chinese government banned the selling of human organs, but there are rumours that the practice continues.

For any family faced with the death of a loved one who desperately needs an organ transplant, it must be tempting to try to get an organ from anywhere, at any price. Yet if that means a healthy person selling part of their body, or a criminal being executed to order somewhere in the world, is the price too high?

"The right to life becomes meaningless when the law forbids you to buy an organ that protects your life."

The Economist

"If you legalise the organ trade, then can you imagine people buying and selling parts of their body because they are too poor. What a horrific situation."

Colin Gonsalves, Human Rights Law Network

LUCY'S STORY

Organ transplantation has always been an uncertain science. Even today, with all our knowledge and technology, transplants fail both immediately after they have been carried out and years later. This uncertainty is hard for doctors who cannot predict which transplants will be successful and which will not. It is much harder for the patients and their families, who have to live with that uncertainty every single day. The story of Lucy Sheehan shows what it is like to be on the receiving end of transplant surgery.

Picking up the problem

Lucy was an alert and endearing baby, but she grew rather slowly so she was given regular check-ups by a **paediatrician**. She seemed to be doing well until, when she was two, her doctor felt that Lucy's liver was enlarged and suggested a scan. The results of the scan were frightening. Lucy's liver was fibrous and scarred – it looked as if she had **cirrhosis** of the liver, a disease more usually found in alcoholics! The family was quickly referred to King's College Hospital in London, one of the top centres for research into liver disease. The doctors didn't know why Lucy's liver wasn't working properly. Because she seemed so well, they decided that the best thing to do was to give her regular check-ups every three months.

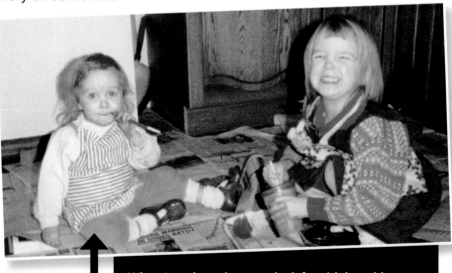

When Lucy (seen here on the left, with her older sister) was two, she appeared to be a normal, lively toddler. It took a whole battery of tests to find out what was going on inside her liver.

With six children, life was pretty hectic in the Sheehan household and there wasn't much time to brood about what might happen next. But just two weeks later the consultant rang Amanda with very bad news. More results from Lucy's tests had shown something abnormal. By the summer, when she was two and a half, the doctors finally arrived at a diagnosis: Lucy not only had cirrhosis of the liver, she also had cells that were becoming cancerous and she needed a liver transplant as soon as possible. The longer she waited the more likely it was that cancer would develop and spread beyond the liver. Without a transplant the doctors said she had about two years to live. In September 1991 Lucy officially went on the list of children waiting for a liver transplant.

> "It was like being on a terrifying emotional roller coaster ride. We never knew what we would have to deal with next. To be told that your two-year-old child might not live to be four – we just went completely cold ..."
>
> Amanda Sheehan, Lucy's mum

The long wait

Ideally, Lucy needed an immediate transplant. But donor organs are not available just when they are needed. The family knew that as they waited, Lucy's chances of survival were ebbing away. Amanda even appeared on national television to make an appeal for people to think about donating organs if their loved ones died. A couple of weeks later they received a call from the hospital to say a donor organ was available. Lucy was prepared for surgery but there was another little girl in need of a liver, and she already had cancer. Her need was greater and so she got the organ. Lucy and her family continued to wait.

The transplant

More time went by without an organ becoming available. After eight months Amanda and Lucy went on television again to raise the profile of people needing transplants. In that week alone, nine transplant operations were carried out on children as donor organs were made available and one of those children was Lucy.

On 13 June, the call came through to say a donor organ had been found so the whole family drove to King's College Hospital. Lucy's brothers and sisters said goodbye to her that night, knowing they might not see her alive again. On 14 June the operation went ahead. Lucy was given one lobe of the liver of an older child.

At just three and a half, Lucy was young and couldn't understand why she had come to hospital feeling fine and now felt so poorly. She needed nine different medicines daily to prevent her body rejecting the new liver. After six weeks in hospital she went home, only for her body to start to reject the liver. Shaking, with a high temperature, she was rushed back into hospital as an emergency. The doctors were not surprised – most children who receive a new organ react like this. But once the rejection was under control Lucy went home again and this time she recovered well.

The intervals between her check-ups got longer and longer as her new liver continued to work well. But it wasn't all plain sailing. In the first two years after her transplant Lucy had a number of infections that caused major problems because of the immuno-suppressant drugs she had to take. However, Lucy and her family just kept going and their persistence paid off. Lucy is still fit and well today. She needs to take a low dose of immuno-suppressant medicine and has one major check-up each year. She is preparing to go to university to read English and Philosophy after travelling around Europe with a friend. Her transplant – almost 16 years ago – has been an amazing success.

The liver that saved Lucy's life was donated by the family of a 12-year-old boy who died during an operation on a tumour in his brain. No-one had expected him to die, and doctors did not ask his stunned parents for permission to use their son's organs. It was the parents themselves who volunteered their son as a donor, in the midst of their own devastation. Their generosity allowed Lucy to live.

"I'm so grateful to my donor. My liver doesn't feel different or strange – it just feels like part of me. I feel completely normal."

Lucy Sheehan, transplant patient

Lucy Sheehan is now a fit, active young woman, planning to go to university. She joins in all the same activities as her friends and relatives. She is a real transplant success story.

PUSHING THE BOUNDARIES

Every 27 minutes, someone somewhere in the world receives an organ transplant. But every couple of hours, someone dies, waiting for an organ donor to turn up. There are simply not enough donor organs available for all the people who need them, and the problem seems to be getting worse rather than better.

As surgical techniques and immuno-suppressant drugs have improved, transplant surgery is seen as the answer to more and more medical problems. At the same time, the introduction of laws making it compulsory to wear seat belts, a reduction in drinking and driving, and improved car safety standards means fewer people are being killed in road accidents. Doctors are able to save the lives of more people who are rushed into hospital. These improvements are welcomed by everyone, but the inevitable side-effect is a reduction in the pool of potential organ donors.

Organs are released from only about 20 per cent of potential donors. Whatever is done to raise people's awareness of the importance of organ transplantation and the need for donors, the supply of donor organs from people who have died will never match the number of people needing transplants. Living donors are being used increasingly, but they too are a very limited resource. It is because of this mismatch of supply and demand that research has been going on into alternative ways of providing organs for transplantation.

Xenotransplantation

One area of research that has received a great deal of media attention and funding is **xenotransplantation**. This is the transplantation into people of organs from other species of animals. Xenotransplantation is not actually a new science. In 1906, a French surgeon, Mathieu Jaboulay, implanted a pig's kidney into one woman and a goat's liver into another. Both women died. But in recent years scientists have begun to think that the use of xenotransplants could solve two of the biggest problems of transplant surgery: the shortage of donor organs and the problems of rejection.

Most of the research into using animals as a source of organs for human transplants has been done using baboons and pigs. Baboons are genetically very close to human beings, so the idea was that rejection problems would probably be relatively small. Physically, too, the organs would fit easily into a person. In 1964, six patients received baboon kidneys; in 1984, a baboon heart was transplanted into a baby girl; in 1992, two patients received baboon livers. All of the patients died within weeks of their operations, but they did not die because they had rejected their new organ. The high dosages of immuno-suppressant drugs they needed to take left them highly vulnerable to infections, and they died of these. However, baboons are not an ideal source of organs because they reproduce very slowly, having only one baby at a time. They also carry many viruses that could be passed on to the human recipient. When animals are used as a source of organs for human transplants, the animals are always killed. Because baboons are so similar to humans, both in the way they look and behave and in their biology, many people have ethical objections to using them as "donors" in this way.

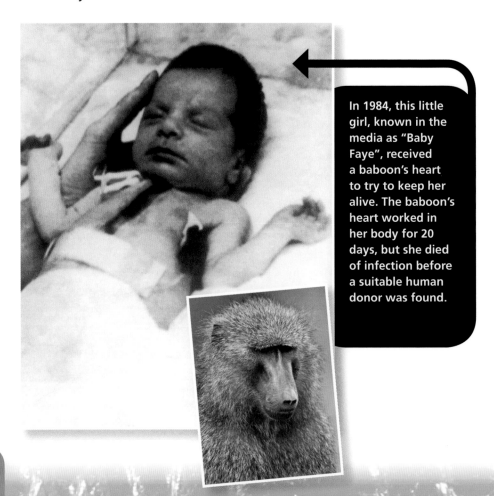

In 1984, this little girl, known in the media as "Baby Faye", received a baboon's heart to try to keep her alive. The baboon's heart worked in her body for 20 days, but she died of infection before a suitable human donor was found.

WHAT ABOUT A PIG'S HEART?

As potential organ sources, pigs have been the main focus of research. Despite the difference in body shape, the anatomy of a pig is amazingly like that of a human. They carry fewer viruses than baboons, and are much easier to breed, producing lots of piglets in each litter. Moral objections to using pigs are also fewer because they are killed for food anyway. The hope among researchers is that, using the techniques of **genetic engineering**, pigs may be modified so they produce hearts, livers, kidneys, and other organs that carry neutral human antigens. This would mean the new organs would not be recognized by the human recipient as foreign tissue. The hope is that genetically modified pigs grown in a sterile environment might provide a virtually unlimited supply of disease-free "human" organs for transplants, and that the recipients would need little or no immuno-suppressant drugs, as the new organs would be recognized by their immune system as "self".

Genetically modified pigs to be used for organ transplants would not be able to live in a natural environment like this. They would need to be reared in a very sterile, bio-medical environment. However, this raises animal welfare issues. Would it be fair to treat these intelligent animals in this way?

DISCUSS Xenotransplantation

What are the big advantages of using animals to provide organs for human beings? Patients need never again die waiting for a donor organ. There would always be suitable organs available, and the problem of rejection could be removed. It sounds a wonderful solution to the problem – so what are the drawbacks of xenotransplantation?

There are a number of ethical objections, not least because animals cannot give consent for the use of their organs, so they cannot be referred to as donors – they are organ sources. Also, the animals would have to be kept in very unnatural, sterile conditions.

The other major problem is the risk of disease. Like all animals, including ourselves, baboons and pigs carry a wide range of viruses – although pigs have fewer than baboons. Many of these are relatively harmless in the baboon or the pig, but any of them could cause a fatal disease in a human host. An example is the virus that causes **AIDS**. It is a relatively harmless virus in monkeys but has devastating effects on people. No one knows if xenotransplants would bring new and deadly diseases into the human race – but it is a very big risk to take.

"The potential for infectious agents to be passed from the source animal, via the transplant, to a human recipient and from the patient into the wider population is still a major concern ... Until such time as research is able to produce more definitive answers on safety ... it is prudent to assume that all forms of xenotransplantation carry a risk of some degree."

Third annual report of the UK Xenotransplantation Interim Regulatory Authority

A large amount of money has been ploughed into research on xenotransplantation, and pigs carrying human genes have been bred in the UK and elsewhere. However, the feeling increasingly seems to be that this will not be the answer, that there are too many problems to be overcome in xenotransplantation, and that other areas of research will come up with the best solution for the shortage of donor organs.

"There has been a lot of scientific hype, leading people to believe that successful animal transplants are just around the corner. But now the regulator is saying that this is not the case and there are serious concerns about safety ..."

Sarah Kite, British Union for the Abolition of Vivisection

Curing diabetes

Diabetes affects millions of people around the world. It can be controlled by injecting insulin, but there is currently no cure. The most promising area of xenotransplantation research is the use of tissue from pigs to cure diabetes. Researchers at the University of Minnesota, USA, are in the forefront of work, using the islet tissue from pigs (the cells that make insulin in the body) to actually cure diabetes. They placed pig islets in monkeys with diabetes and the animals started to make insulin and no longer needed injections. They needed strong immuno-suppressant drugs but the monkeys have survived, diabetes free, for many months. Other scientists are now working on ways to reduce the need for the immuno-suppressants by enclosing the pig cells in capsules that do not trigger the immune response. Doctors and scientists hope that human trials are not far off.

Tissue engineering

One of the other advances in medicine that can only become more important in the future is **tissue engineering**, the process of growing body organs in the lab. It has already been done by Dr Charles Vacanti in 1997, when he grew a human ear on the back of a mouse. A mould in the shape of an ear was made of biodegradable material and implanted onto the mouse's back. Then, human cartilage cells were placed over the mould. They eventually grew into a non-hearing human ear, which was successfully removed without killing the mouse. This was one of the first successes in using tissue engineering to form an organ.

The procedure that is furthest along in development is the growth of human bladders. This is because bladder cells can be grown outside the human body. Dr Anthony Atala, working at Wake Forest University in the United States, says that the best and quickest option is if the cells can be taken from the actual patient. Any issues of rejection can then be avoided. In 1999, seven patients were given artificial bladders that had been grown in the laboratory.

Tissue engineering is still in its infancy and is concentrating on the simpler tissues such as cartilage, skin, and vascular tissues. Heart valves and blood vessels are being developed. Obviously, safety is of paramount importance so the trials are moving slowly but the hope is that more complex organs, such as the liver, will be engineered at some point in the future.

RESEARCH – THE CUTTING EDGE

The number of people waiting for an organ transplant around the world is large, and it is growing. In the UK, there are almost 7,000 people waiting for transplants, and in Australia the numbers are similar. About 44,000 Americans are on the waiting lists, yet only 18,270 operations were carried out in the year 2000. It was hoped that xenotransplantation would provide a ready supply of organs, but at the same time as those hopes faded, new discoveries were being made that may well be the answer to the organ shortage in the future.

FOCUS The pluripotent stem cell

Stem cells divide and form the specialized cells of the body that make up the various tissues and organs. When an egg and sperm fuse to form an embryo, those early cells will eventually give rise to every type of cell in the adult human body. By the stage at which the embryo would implant in its mothers womb it has become a hollow ball of cells. The inner cells of this ball are what is known as pluripotent, because they will eventually form most, but not all, of the cells of the baby. These pluripotent stem cells get even more specialized as the embryo develops, forming, for example, blood stem cells that give rise to blood cells and skin stem cells that in turn give rise to skin cells.

This human embryo is at the eight cell stage. In the right conditions in the womb this small group of cells can form all the organs of the human body. Now scientists may be able to harness and use that potential.

In 1998, in a breakthrough that caused ripples of excitement through the scientific and medical world, two American scientists managed to **culture** human embryonic stem cells that were still pluripotent. James Thomson and his research team at the University of Wisconsin in the United States maintained a culture of human embryonic stem cells for several months. They originally got the cells from spare embryos that had been produced during *in vitro* **fertilization** treatments. Couples had donated their spare embryos for scientific research, rather than simply having them destroyed.

At the same time, John Gearhart and his group at Johns Hopkins University in the United States were also culturing human embryonic stem cells, from a slightly different part of the embryo. The cells used by John Gearhart came from foetuses that had been aborted after five to nine weeks of development.

James Thomson has been involved in two major breakthroughs in recent years. First, he cultured stem cells and then, in 2008, he announced that he had reprogrammed adult skin cells.

Why so much excitement?

The culturing of embryonic stem cells has caused a major stir. In theory at least, the pluripotent cells could be encouraged to grow into almost any different type of cell needed in the body. They could provide an amazing variety of cures for diseases and other medical problems. For example, they could provide new nerve cells for people with brain disorders or spinal injuries, new heart muscle cells to repair hearts damaged by heart attacks, and new and effective treatments for **strokes**, burns, and **arthritis**. For those people waiting desperately for a transplant, the hope is that it may be possible to produce whole new organs by growing the stem cells in the right conditions. This means there may be a potentially limitless source of donor organs. It could also revolutionize the treatment of many other diseases and change the testing of drugs, reducing the need for animal experiments.

At the moment, no one is quite sure just how the cells in an embryo are switched on or off to form particular types of tissue – kidney rather than liver, or liver rather than heart. As the answers to these questions are found, the potential will be there for a limitless supply of new organs. Not only that, but the problem of rejection could be solved. The immune system does not attack and destroy a developing embryo, even though it has different antigens on its cells to those of the mother. Perhaps new cells or organs created from embryo stem cells will enjoy this same protection.

Alternatives to embryos

Research into stem cells has spread out in a number of different ways, many of which attempt to avoid the use of the most controversial, embryo derived cells.

CLONING, UMBILICAL CORDS, AND ADULT BODIES

One alternative is to take an empty human egg and place the nucleus of an adult cell inside it. An "embryo" develops that has nothing to do with normal reproduction. It is actually a clone of someone who already exists. This clone can then be used as a source of embryonic stem cells for research.

Blood from the umbilical cord (which joins the developing baby to the mother's placenta in the uterus) of newborn babies contains embryonic stem cells and these could help to overcome some of the reservations. It may become possible to store stem cells from every newborn baby ready for when they might need them later in their lives. These stem cells are not quite as good as cells from the early embryo but they have huge potential to form other body cell types.

Scientists are also finding some stem cells in adults that appear to have the ability to grow into several different types of tissue. There seem to be more limitations with these adult stem cells than with embryonic ones, because they seem limited in the cell types they can develop into. However, this is another possible way forward that could avoid both rejection problems and the controversial use of embryonic tissue.

Harvesting embryonic stem cells from the umbilical cords of newborn babies could avoid the use of tissue from early embryos and overcome ethical problems.

Reprogramming cells

In one very exciting new development, teams of scientists in Japan and the United States have reprogrammed adult skin cells to become pluripotent stem cells again. Known as iPS or induced pluripotent stem cells, these cells show most of the characteristics of normal embryonic stem cells. The technique involved changing four genes in the original adult cells. The genes were altered using genetic engineering (genetic modification), with the desired genes carried into the cell using viruses.

The cells produced can be used to generate different types of adult cells. However, there are still many hurdles to overcome with this work. The new cells carry the viruses used to engineer them and they cannot form all of the cells types needed. This work offers another way in which the shortage of donor organs and tissues may be overcome in the future.

DISCUSS   The ethical stumbling block

The major ethical problem with research into pluripotent cells is that they come either from aborted embryos or from spare embryos in fertility treatment. There are many people, including many religious groups, who feel it is wrong to use a potential human being as a source of material in this way. It is also argued that the embryo cannot give permission so using it is a violation of its human rights. The research is so controversial that funding was stopped for a time in the United States until the situation had been discussed in detail. Eventually the US government decided that from August 2001 such work could continue on human pluripotent cells provided they met certain strict criteria.

In the UK there was also considerable debate before legislation was passed to extend the Human Fertilization and Embryology Act to allow embryonic stem cell research to take place. European Union legislation also controls tightly what may be done with these cells.

Continued ...

"Federal funds may be awarded for research using human embryonic stem cells if the following criteria are met:
• The derivation process (which begins with the destruction of the embryo) was initiated prior to 9:00 P.M. EDT on 9th August, 2001.
• The stem cells must have been derived from an embryo that was created for reproductive purposes and was no longer needed.
• Informed consent must have been obtained for the donation of the embryo and that donation must not have involved financial inducements."

George W. Bush, 9 August 2001

All of this groundbreaking science raises moral and ethical questions. For example, even something that sounds relatively simple like the storage of umbilical cord blood raises problems. Imagine the space needed to store all the blood from every baby born – and would this be a service only available to wealthy people who will be able to afford to pay for the storage?

Other more complex issues can end up decided by law. One of the problems with stem cell research is a shortage of human eggs to use in cloning. Scientists in the UK came up with an alternative. They used empty cows' eggs, and to each egg added the nucleus of an adult human cell. This then started to divide to form an early embryo of effectively human cells that could be used in research, leaving human eggs for reproductive technology. This process caused uproar with some people who felt it was completely unethical both because it involved an "embryo" and because it mixed human and animal tissue. After a great deal of debate, Parliament passed a law making this type of experimentation possible. Many people celebrated the opportunity to seek out the answers to some of the most unpleasant human diseases. Others were still very unhappy on ethical grounds. What decision would you have made?

INTO THE FUTURE

The field of organ transplantation is an exciting and ever-moving one. Surgeons are continually looking for new techniques that will make transplants more effective and enable more organs to be transplanted. For example, the use of parts of both lungs and livers in transplants has made it easier to use live donors, and has meant that more people can be helped by a single dead donor.

Drug companies are working towards new drugs to help with the problem of rejection. In particular, they are trying to develop drugs that suppress the part of the immune system that causes the rejection of a transplanted organ without suppressing the body's natural defence against disease. The ideal scenario of all transplant research is to develop rejection-free transplants.

Although there are constant innovations, not all of them are successful. In the 1970s, Robert Jarvik designed an artificial heart that he hoped would be able to function long-term in the human body, removing the need for human donors and avoiding problems of rejection. A number of these artificial hearts were transplanted and one patient, William Schroeder, lived for 620 days. However, the quality of life for these patients was not very good, and they suffered many infections and other problems. Eventually, doctors decided that the only real use for artificial hearts was to provide a bridge to a human transplant, prolonging a patient's life in the hope that a suitable donor might be found.

In the year 2000, the British surgeon Stephen Westaby, based in Oxford, implanted a much smaller device, the Jarvik 2000, into the left ventricle (pumping chamber) of a patient's heart. This supported the function of the failing heart, helping to pump the blood effectively around the body, and the patient lived another five months. Since then, more implants like these have taken place. The hope for the future is that a tiny implant will replace the need for a full heart transplant.

How far can we go?

The idea of transplant surgery has grown and developed from a very experimental science in the last century to a well accepted treatment for many different forms of organ failure today. In 2005, doctors carried out the first face transplant on Isabelle Dinoire, a French woman who had been savagely attacked by a dog. The transplant was successful, but doctors are moving slowly in this area and there are many psychological problems to overcome when the appearance of a person is changed in this way.

A face transplant has revolutionized Isabelle's life and the advances that made this possible may help many other people in the future.

"Carrying a donor card is rather like carrying a credit card, except that you are offering other people the chance of life. I wish everyone would carry one."

Lucy Sheehan, successful transplant patient

Developments with stem cells mean that within your lifetime, not only might the shortage of organ donors be overcome but so might the problems of rejection. Drug-free transplants available as soon as they are needed by the patient are the ideal that doctors are working towards.

There are still problems that transplantation cannot overcome. If someone is severely brain damaged in an accident, such that their brain stem dies, their organs can be used to offer hope of new life to others – but the process cannot be reversed. Doctors cannot transplant a new brain and restore life within the damaged body.

However, there are many ways in which transplant medicine is a triumph of human endeavour. It can be used to help people of all ages. Tiny babies, children, teenagers, adults – even relatively elderly people in their seventies – have been given new kidneys and other organs that have restored their quality of life. Nothing can ease the loss of a loved one for donor families, but they do have the knowledge that their relative has helped others to live. Taking a dying person and restoring them to health using the organs of another person seems almost unbelievable – organ transplantation is a modern miracle of medicine.

TIMELINE

800 BC

Susrata, a surgeon in India, is reputed to have grafted new noses from skin flaps.

1962

The first successful kidney transplant using a dead donor is carried out in the United States. The kidney functions for 21 months.

1959

Doctors Murray and Merrill carry out the first successful human kidney allograft between non-identical twins.

1963

The first lung transplant is carried out by Dr James Hardy in the United States.

Bone marrow is transplanted for the first time, leading to a revolution in the treatment of cancers such as leukaemia.

1966

A successful pancreas transplant is carried out for the first time in the United States.

1992

The first baboon to human liver transplant is carried out in the United States. The recipient lives for 70 days.

First pig to human liver transplant. The recipient dies after two days.

1989

The first successful liver transplant from a living relative takes place in the United States.

The first transplant of a complete small intestine takes place.

1987

The first domino transplant takes place.

Dr Starzl is involved in the first successful transplant of several different abdominal organs.

1996

The first successful split-liver transplants take place — using the liver from a dead donor to give more than one recipient the chance of life.

1998

Human embryonic stem cells are cultured in the laboratory for the first time in the United States.

200 AD

The first recorded reference to the concept of organ transplantation is made around this time — Hua-To in China is reported to have replaced diseased organs with healthy ones.

1954

The first successful human kidney transplant takes place in the United States between identical twin brothers. The transplanted kidney works for eight years.

1940s

Sir Peter Medawar and others begin to understand and explain the human immune system.

1902

The first successful kidney transplant (in a dog) is carried out by Emerich Ullman.

1967

The first really successful liver transplant is carried out by Dr Thomas Starzl in the United States. The liver functions for 13 months.

The first successful human heart transplant is carried out by Dr Christiaan Barnard in South Africa. The heart functions for 18 days.

1969

The fungus *Beauveria nivea* is discovered, which leads to the finding of cyclosporine in the United States and Norway.

1972

Jean Borel discovers the immuno-suppressant properties of cyclosporine.

1984

"Baby Faye" in the United States is given a baboon's heart, which works for 20 days.

1983

Cyclosporine is approved for use as an immuno-suppressant drug.

1982

The first artificial heart, the Jarvik 7, is transplanted into Barney Clarke.

1981

The first successful heart/lung transplant takes place in the United States. The new organs function for five years.

1980

Cyclosporine is first synthesized

2000

The second Jarvik artificial heart (Jarvik 2000) is first used. The patient lives for five months.

2005

The first face transplant was carried out on a French woman, Isabelle Dinoire, whose face had been savaged by a dog.

2007–2008

Using genetic engineering, scientists reprogrammed skin cells so that they behaved like pluripotent stem cells again.

GLOSSARY

abdominal organs organs found in the abdomen, for example the digestive system and the kidneys

ABO system classification system for blood. It identifies four major blood types.

AIDS (acquired immune deficiency syndrome) condition caused by the HIV virus in which the immune system is severely weakened, leaving the patient vulnerable to diseases such as pneumonia and tuberculosis, from which the patient eventually dies

air sacs tiny spaces in the lungs where gas exchange takes place

antibodies special proteins made by the immune system that attach to any foreign antigens and inactivate the invading cell

antigens special marker molecules sticking out from the surface of cell membranes

arthritis inflammation of the joints, a condition that is often very painful and can be crippling

bone marrow soft tissue in the hollow sections of the bones where blood is made

cancer potentially fatal disease caused by the uncontrolled growth of cells

carbohydrates type of food molecule that acts as an energy source

carbon dioxide gas produced as a waste product of respiration by most living organisms

central nervous system linked system of nerves, including the brain and spinal cord, which carry electrical messages around the body

cholesterol type of fat that is present in most body tissues. It is thought to be involved in many forms of heart disease.

cirrhosis disease of the liver, often caused by excess alcohol intake, where the liver function is progressively lost due to fibrous tissues replacing normal liver cells

conception moment at which a sperm and an egg join together to create an embryo

culture to grow micro-organisms or cells in the laboratory

cyclosporine drug that damps down the reaction of the immune system to foreign cells

domino transplants transplants that have a knock-on effect, providing organs for two recipients. A patient with diseased lungs but a healthy heart receives a heart/lung transplant, and their healthy heart is then donated to a patient needing a heart transplant.

donor someone who donates an organ (either when they are alive, or promised after their death) to help someone who lacks this organ

embryo very early stages of human development in the uterus

ethical relating to what is morally right

fertilize to join a male and female sex cell together to form a new individual

fungus type of organism that produces spores, includes moulds, yeast, and mushrooms

genetic diseases diseases that occur because of defects in the genes or chromosomes

genetic engineering process by which the genetic material of a cell may be altered either by replacing damaged genetic material or adding extra genetic material

graft to transplant a piece of tissue from one place on a person's body to another place, either on the same body or someone else's

heart attack when blood flow to the heart is reduced due to a blockage in the blood vessel, causing a sudden abnormality in the functioning of the heart

immune system system in the body that recognizes foreign cells and destroys them

immuno-suppressant causing a reduction in the activity of the immune system

in vitro fertilization medical treatment in which an egg is fertilized outside of the body of the mother before being returned to her uterus

infection invasion of the body by micro-organisms

kidney organ that removes waste urea and excess salt from the blood, producing urine which is passed into the bladder

lymphocytes white blood cells that make antibodies

membrane thin layer or "skin" around cells

micro-organisms organisms, like bacteria, that are too small to see with the naked eye and need to be viewed through a microscope

molecule tiny particle, made up of more than one atom joined together

organ systems collection of organs working together to carry out a major function in the body

paediatrician doctor who specializes in children's diseases

placenta organ in the mother's uterus that supplies a developing baby with food and oxygen

protein type of food molecule important for muscle-building and growth

recipient patient who receives a donated organ

rejection to refuse to accept; rejection of transplanted organs occurs when the body realizes they are not its own

scan way of looking into the body without opening it up. Different types of scan can be used in the diagnosis of disease and monitoring of health.

steroids lipid-based chemical. Some hormones are steroids and steroid drugs are used for a variety of reasons.

strokes sudden interruption of the brain's blood supply caused by the rupture of a blood vessel or a clot formation in the brain. These can damage the body's functioning and even cause death.

synthesize to make. Chemicals can be made artificially rather than extracted from a source (for example an organism).

tissue collection of cells in the body that all carry out the same function, for example muscle tissue

tissue engineering process of growing body organs in the laboratory

toxin (toxic) poison (something that is poisonous)

urea toxic chemical made when excess protein is broken down in the body

uterus female organ in which the foetus develops

xenotransplantation transplanting an organ from one species of animal into a different species

FIND OUT MORE

Further reading

Cutting Edge Medicine: Organ Transplantation, Carol Ballard (Franklin Watts, 2007)

Human Physiology and Health, David Wright (Heinemann Educational, 2007)

Science in the News: Organ Transplantation, Andrew Campbell (Franklin Watts, 2008)

Why Science Matters: Repairing and Replacing Organs, Andrew Solway (Heinemann Library, 2008)

Websites

www.uktransplant.org.uk/ukt/how_to_become_a_donor/ questions/questions.jsp
This web page answers any questions you may have about being an organ donor.

http://ukhealthcare.uky.edu/transplant
The UK HealthCare Transplant Centre has been carrying out organ transplants since 1964. Their website includes an explanation of the different types of transplants, a glossary of terms, and patients' stories.

www.chron.com/content/chronicle/special/transplant/history.html
This link gives a timeline of transplant history from 1933 to 1986. During these years the major breakthroughs in human transplantation were made, including the transplantation of kidneys, livers, and hearts. The introduction of drugs that helped patients to retain transplanted organs and the establishment of national databases of donors also figure in this chart of transplantation developments.

INDEX